IMAGES
of Sports

THE
BOSTON GARDEN

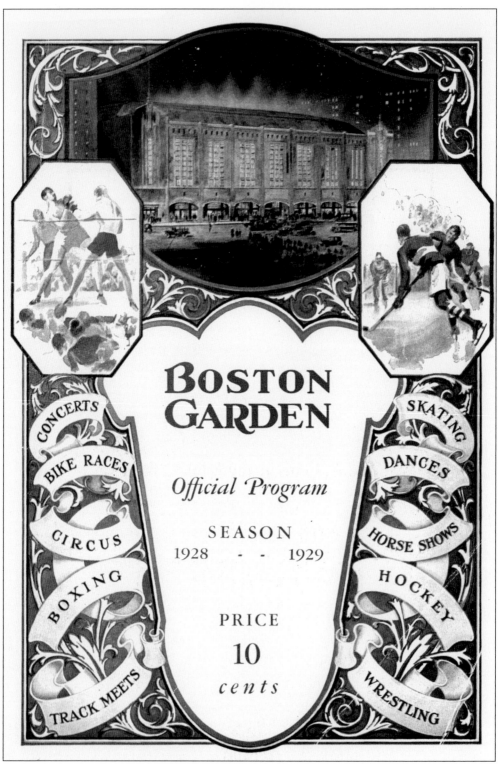

BOSTON GARDEN

Official Program

SEASON
1928 - - 1929

PRICE
10
cents

CONCERTS

BIKE RACES

CIRCUS

BOXING

TRACK MEETS

SKATING

DANCES

HORSE SHOWS

HOCKEY

WRESTLING

Seen here is a program from the Boston Garden's first year.

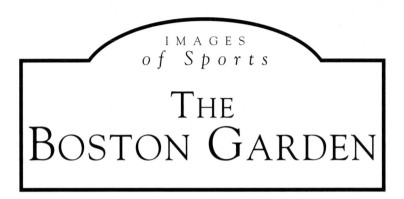

IMAGES
of Sports

THE
BOSTON GARDEN

Richard A. Johnson and Brian Codagnone

ARCADIA

First printed in 2002.
Reprinted in 2003.

Published by Arcadia Publishing,
an imprint of Tempus Publishing, Inc.
2A Cumberland Street
Charleston, SC 29401

Printed in Great Britain.

Library of Congress Catalog Card Number: 2002113434

For all general information contact Arcadia Publishing at:
Telephone 843-853-2070
Fax 843-853-0044
E-Mail sales@arcadiapublishing.com

For customer service and orders:
Toll-Free 1-888-313-2665

Visit us on the internet at http://www.arcadiapublishing.com

*To Rich Krezwick, FleetCenter president and chief executive
officer, for his belief in, and loyal support of, the Sports Museum.*

*To Mary Hamilton Johnson for her courage
and grace under pressure.*

—R.A.J.

To my family.

—B.C.

Authors' note: Proceeds from the sale of this book will benefit the Sports Museum of New
England at the FleetCenter, Boston.

CONTENTS

ACKNOWLEDGMENTS

I wish to thank my coauthor Brian Codagnone for his superb job of research on both the text and illustrations for this volume. He serves the museum as associate curator and operations coordinator at our FleetCenter home and is also a professional cartoonist and graphic artist.

We are grateful to the staffs of both the FleetCenter and Sports Museum for their assistance with this project. Thanks go to Jeremy Jacobs (FleetCenter chair), Rich Krezwick (executive director), John Wentzell, Jim Bednarek, Peter Webber, Tina Anderson, Chris Maher, Amy Lattimer, Jim Delaney, Roman "Rusty" Rustia, Courtney McIlhenny, Nate Greenburg, Heidi Holland, Joe Curnane, Sue Byrne, Armando Madeira and the carpentry crew, and many others. Malcolm Graham (Sports Museum chair), Bill Galatis (executive director), Michelle Gormley (education director), M.J. Coyne (intern), Dave Cowens (trustee), Adam Hansen, Kami Medeiros, and Gordon Katz also offered support.

Special thanks go to Bruins photographers Al Ruelle and Steve and Brian Babineau for their generous support. Likewise, thanks go to Celtics photographers Dick Raphael and Steve Lipofsky. Aaron Schmidt of the Boston Public Library print department also helped, as did Harvey McKenney, John Brooks, Mac McDiarmid, Bill Swift, Phil Castinetti, Ruth Mack O'Toole, Michele Lee Amundsen, Mark Torpey and John Cronin of the Boston Herald, Joe Sullivan of the Boston Globe, Frank O'Brien, and Ken Gloss of Boston's venerable Brattle Book Store.

INTRODUCTION

My memories of the Boston Garden include a plethora of images and impressions. The walk up Canal Street from Haymarket always set the tone for any Garden event. On a winter night, it resembled the set of a 1930s gangster film, like *Public Enemy* or *Angels with Dirty Faces*. At every corner, characters from a real-life version of *The Friends of Eddie Coyle* hustled tickets and parking spaces. In the decade that Bobby Orr and Phil Esposito led the "Big Bad Bruins," more than a few of these hucksters sent their kids to Boston College and Harvard on the lucre reaped from scalped tickets.

In sharp contrast, choice seats for the championship-winning Celtics of the Cousy-Russell and Havlicek-Cowens eras were almost always available on the day of the game for face value at the box office. In fact, for several years, the team scheduled doubleheaders with the likes of Somerville High School and other NBA teams to boost attendance. Go figure.

In its 67 years, the Boston Garden served the region as a sports arena, cathedral, music hall, revival tent, smoky political backroom, nightclub, convention hall, gladiatorial stage, and de facto community center. Not only did the Garden fulfill all these and many other roles, it often served them more than twice in the span of a day with countless afternoon and evening hockey and basketball competitions and other event changeovers. For most of its history, the Garden's hardest working team was the bull gang charged with transforming the ice to flooring and back again in the span of several hours.

The Boston Garden was our version of Shakespeare's famed Globe Theater—namely, a venue where all strata of society gathered to watch a game, hear a speech, or simply dance in the stairways. It was here that thousands learned of the attack on Pearl Harbor during a Boston Olympics matinee. Five years later, a 27-year-old decorated combat veteran named John F. Kennedy also attended Olympics hockey games with his friend Dave Powers to plot the strategy that launched his political career with victory in the 8th district congressional race of 1946 (won on the same night another Celtic dynasty was born, as the Celtics played the first regular season home game in their history).

It was here where several generations of fans enjoyed community skating, police and firemen's balls, fundraisers for Israel as well as Catholic missions, and legendary political rallies such as those for Roosevelt, Curley, Saltonstall, Dewey, Eisenhower, and Kennedy. It was also here that boxing superstar Joe Louis defended his heavyweight crown against Al McCoy in 1940 and an obscure young hurdler from Williams College named George Steinbrenner chased glory in the 1950 Boston Athletic Association (BAA) track meet. Ask any New Englander about their most treasured Garden memory and prepare yourself for an equal measure of stories of events witnessed by, and events featuring, the storyteller as participant.

Long before the advent of sports and event marketing men such as George V. Brown, son Walter Brown and Eddie Powers realized that by simply making their building an accessible and affordable people's palace they would create both wealth and goodwill. Their building was our building, and for three generations, the Boston Garden was as intimate and animated as a local tavern on payday or family dining room on Thanksgiving Day.

—Richard A. Johnson
September 2002

One

THE 1920s

NORTH STATION AT THE TURN OF THE CENTURY. This elegant facade graced the train station in the Victorian era. (Courtesy Richard A. Johnson.)

The Boston Garden Block under Construction. Taken from the Custom House tower, this 1928 photograph shows 150 Causeway Street rising (right), the Boston Garden (center), and an empty space (left), where the Hotel Manger, later known as the Hotel Madison, was to be built. (Courtesy Massachusetts Historical Society.)

A Ticket from the First Event at the Boston Garden, November 17, 1928. The Boxing Carnival featured a non-championship bout between featherweights Dick "Honeyboy" Finnegan of Dorchester and Andre Routis of France. (Courtesy the Sports Museum.)

TEX RICKARD. Promoter extraordinaire Tex Rickard (on the right with a cane) was the original developer and owner of the Boston Garden. Planning a series of six "Gardens" across the country, Rickard had the arena built to specifications similar to Madison Square Garden in New York, which he also operated. His master plan came to a sudden halt when he died just months after the Boston Garden was completed. (Courtesy the Sports Museum.)

A Night View of the Boston Garden. This 1920s time-exposure photograph shows the view down Canal Street, looking toward the distinctive facade of the Garden. The elevated track still serves the Lechmere branch of the Massachusetts Bay Transit Authority's (MBTA) Green Line. Note the streetcar tracks in the road. (Courtesy the Sports Museum.)

"HONEYBOY" FINNEGAN. Dorchester native "Honeyboy" Finnegan fought world featherweight champion Andre Routis in a 10-round decision on the opening night of Boston Garden. Although it was not a title fight, 14,000 fans showed up. Finnegan would later be married at the Boston Garden. (Courtesy the family of Honeyboy Finnegan.)

OPENING NIGHT AT THE BOSTON GARDEN. Referee Jimmy Walsh (center) looks on as local boxer Honeyboy Finnegan (right) beats Andre Routis on November 17, 1928, in the Boston Garden opening night match. Although the Garden would see many sporting events over its lifetime, its primary purpose was as a boxing venue. (Courtesy the family of Honeyboy Finnegan.)

EDDIE SHORE GREETING FANS. In this 1929 photograph, Eddie Shore signs autographs before practice at the Boston Garden. (Courtesy the Sports Museum.)

DIT CLAPPER AND EDDIE SHORE. Shown here at the beginning of his long career, Dit Clapper (left) was both the National Hockey League's and the Bruins' first 20-year man. Clapper captained the Bruins for 14 seasons, still a club record. However, it was his leadership off the ice that made Clapper the consummate team man. He displayed to all Bruin hopefuls the pride and character of the black and gold and served as a mentor to several generations of Bruins. Eddie Shore (right) was not only the best defenseman of his generation, he was one of the toughest men ever to lace on skates. In a Bruins career that spanned 14 years, he suffered nearly 1,000 stitches, broke his nose 14 times, broke his jaw 5 times, lost most of his teeth, and nearly lost an ear. A four-time most valuable player (MVP) and seven-time first team all-star, Shore played on two Bruins Stanley Cup winners. (Courtesy the Sports Museum.)

THE FIRST BRUINS GAME AT THE BOSTON GARDEN. On November 20, 1928, more than 16,000 fans jammed into the Boston Garden (well beyond capacity) to see the Bruins play Montreal. After a 15-minute delay to allow the fans to push their way to their seats, the Canadiens won the game 1-0 on a goal by Sylvio Mantha. Playing in that game were such stars

as Eddie Shore, Tiny Thompson, Harry Oliver, Lionel Hitchman, Frank Frederickson, Dit Clapper, Howie Morenz, Aurel Joliat, Art Gagne, and George Hainsworth. (Courtesy the Sports Museum.)

A Ticket Stub from the First Bruins Game at the Boston Garden. For the sum of $1.50, fans could see the Bruins play the Montreal Canadiens in the first game in their new home. Having previously played at Boston Arena (now Northeastern University's Matthews Arena), the team had a new home that boasted more seats, modern amenities, and easier access by train and subway. (Courtesy the Sports Museum.)

The First Bruins Team to Play at Boston Garden. This talented team boasted seven future Hockey Hall of Famers. Seen here, from left to right, are the following: (front row) Tiny Thompson, Frank Frederickson, Eddie Shore, Lionel Hitchman, Cy Denneney, Dutch Gainor, and Hal Winkler (who was mistakenly identified as Hal Winkle); (back row) Cooney Weiland, Harry Oliver, Erik Pettinger, Dit Clapper, Lloyd Klein, Percy Galbraith, Eddie Rodden, and Red Green. (Courtesy the Sports Museum.)

Two

THE 1930S

BOSTON GARDEN NEWS. This program
is from the 1930–1931 season.
(Courtesy the Sports Museum.)

A BOSTON GARDEN ARENA AND EXHIBITION HALL PROGRAM. To promote the versatility of their new venue, the Boston Madison Square Garden Corporation produced this booklet. Conventions, shows, circuses, rodeos, concerts, sports events, and more were seen by more than 1.5 million patrons every year, boasted the lavishly illustrated program. The latest in modern amenities and a prime location made the Boston Garden the location of choice for all sorts of activities. (Courtesy the Sports Museum.)

BOSTON GARDEN AS A CATHEDRAL. The Garden was a popular place for evangelical meetings. The building was filled to capacity and then some by the faithful as they listened to the leading religious leaders of the era, such as British evangelist Gipsy Smith and American icon Aime Semple MacPherson. (Courtesy the Sports Museum.)

Golf Bowl

TRADE — MARK
PATENTS PENDING

"THE NAME'S THE GAME"

PLAY THIS FASCINATING GAME AT THE NEW

Boston Garden Golf Course

Played like golf - Scored like bowling

15c

30 balls
10 frames

15ᶜ

30 balls

10 frames

Sales Office:

249
TREMONT ST.
(Opp. Metropolitan Theatre)

BOSTON GARDEN GOLF-BOWLING COURSE. "Played like golf—scored like bowling," bragged this 1930 advertisement for the new game of golf bowl. This precursor of miniature golf was added to the stable of sports and game crazes of the era, although it never achieved popular success. Set up in a bowling-pin pattern were 10 small bottle pins, and players used a putter and golf ball to knock them down. Another game, golfun, combined golf and pool skills. (Courtesy the Sports Museum.)

THE CIRCUS COMES TO TOWN. The Ringling Brothers and Barnum & Bailey Circus was a mainstay at the Garden since it opened. The parade of animals and performers down Tremont Street was an annual event that heralded the arrival of "the Greatest Show on Earth." The so-called elephant ramp, which allowed both animals and trucks access to the Garden, could be pitched only to a specific height or the elephants would not climb it. The FleetCenter access ramp was built at the same angle. (Courtesy the Sports Museum.)

THE TILDEN-KOZELUH TENNIS MATCH. More than 15,000 tennis fans watched superstar "Big Bill" Tilden play Czech champion Karel Kozeluh in the first major indoor tennis match in Boston. (Courtesy the Sports Museum.)

BICYCLE RACING IN THE BOSTON GARDEN. The sports-happy 1920s saw the popularity of many unusual activities, including bicycle racing. The riders circled a banked track on the latest and fastest racing bikes. (Courtesy the Sports Museum.)

THE RODEO. The rodeo was one of the most popular events at Boston Garden. The descendant of such spectacles as Bill Cody's Buffalo Bill's Wild West show, the rodeo brought the West to the city dwellers of the East. A seemingly endless parade of trained horses, cattle roping, trick shooting, and lasso tricks dazzled audiences long before the era of light shows and special effects. (Courtesy the Sports Museum.)

Danno O'Mahoney. Long before Hulk Hogan and the Rock, wrestling packed fans in at the Garden. Such ring luminaries as Gus Sonnenberg, Danno O'Mahoney, Killer Kowalski, Chief Jay Strongbow, Gorgeous George, and others entertained the crowds. (Courtesy the Sports Museum.)

The Hotel Manger. As seen in this 1939 advertisement, the Hotel Manger (later the Hotel Madison) was a modern luxury hotel that provided direct access to the adjacent Garden. The convenient location made it the hotel of choice for visiting teams and celebrities. It was demolished in 1985 to make way for the Tip O'Neill Federal Building. (Courtesy the Sports Museum.)

24

THE SHORE-BAILEY INCIDENT. On the night of December 12, 1933, the Bruins faced the Maple Leafs in Boston. Leading a rush up the ice, Eddie Shore was tripped by Toronto defenseman King Clancy. When no penalty was called, Shore took matters into his own hands. Shore threw a devastating hit at Ace Bailey, who had dropped back to cover for Clancy. Whether he mistook Bailey for Clancy or was just venting his wrath on the first Leaf he saw was never established. Bailey was thrown in the air and hit the ice with such force that nearly everyone in attendance heard the sickening impact. As Bailey lay twitching on the ice, Toronto enforcer Red Horner confronted Shore. When Shore, not realizing how badly he had injured Bailey, just grinned, Horner punched him, knocking him to the ice. He, too, hit his head and lost consciousness. Bailey's life hung in the balance for nearly two weeks. Two delicate operations were required to relieve the blood clots in his brain. He eventually recovered but never played again. Shore received a 16-game suspension but faced no criminal charges. A benefit game was held on February 14, 1934, between the Maple Leafs and a team of NHL all-stars, the precursor of the all-star game (the Bruins also donated the proceeds from a game in Boston to Bailey). Shore and Bailey met and shook hands before the game, Bailey in street clothes and dark glasses, Shore now sporting a helmet. Bailey moved on to a job as an official at Maple Leaf Gardens, and Shore continued to play until 1940. Both players were eventually inducted into the Hockey Hall of Fame. (Courtesy the Sports Museum.)

A U.S. Navy Airship Passes over Boston Garden. In 1928, the U.S. Navy contracted with Goodyear-Zeppelin for the construction of two dirigibles, the *Akron* and the *Macon*. The navy's fleet of rigid airships was never realized. After the *Akron* was wrecked in a storm off New Jersey in 1933 and the *Macon* in a storm off California in 1935, the airship program was abandoned. Previously, the navy airship *Shenandoah* also foundered in a storm. Only the *Los Angeles* survived to be decommissioned. (Courtesy the New Boston Garden Corporation.)

COONEY WEILAND, ART ROSS, DIT CLAPPER, AND EDDIE SHORE. Art Ross, Bruins general manager, confers with three of his star players. Art Ross was the original "Papa Bear" of the Boston Bruins, serving for four decades as a coach, general manager, and resident hockey genius. He coached two Stanley Cup champion teams and introduced innovations such as the bowed hockey net, a smooth-edged puck, and the metal hockey stick. Weiland, along with his Minneapolis Miller teammate Tiny Thompson, joined the Bruins in 1928 and helped lead Boston to their first Stanley Cup. Weiland was also member of the 1939 Stanley Cup champion team and coached Boston to another cup in 1941. He later went on to coach at Harvard for 21 seasons, winning 315 games. (Leslie Jones photograph, courtesy the Sports Museum.)

FRANK BRIMSEK AND EDDIE SHORE. One of the few American players in the NHL at the time, Minnesota's Frank Brimsek replaced the popular Tiny Thompson in the Bruins net in 1938. After losing his debut, he went on to post six shutouts in his first eight games. "Mr. Zero" backboned the Bruins to the Stanley Cup that year, one of two that he would win in Boston. He also won the Vezina Trophy (top goaltender), the Calder Trophy (rookie of the year), and was a first team all-star. (Leslie Jones photograph, courtesy the Sports Museum.)

WALTER BROWN. Walter Brown took over from his father, George V. Brown, as general manager of the Boston Garden in 1937. He held the titles of president of the Boston Garden, chairman of the Basketball Hall of Fame, member of the Hockey Hall of Fame Governing Committee, and president of the International Ice Hockey Federation. Brown was also the founder and owner of the Boston Celtics and co-owner of the Boston Bruins. (Courtesy the Sports Museum.)

AT THE GARDEN SKI PARTY. In December 1935, the Boston Garden played host to a winter exhibition that included sled dogs, skating exhibitions, fashions for the slopes, and a full indoor ski jump. (Gene Mack cartoon, courtesy the Sports Museum.)

A SKI JUMP IN BOSTON GARDEN. The centerpiece of the 1935 Boston Garden Winter Exhibition was an indoor ski jump that was the brainchild of Walter Brown. (Courtesy the Sports Museum.)

JAMES MICHAEL CURLEY RALLY AT THE BOSTON GARDEN. This 1938 political rally packed the Garden with James Michael Curley supporters. The popular and controversial politician served as both mayor of Boston and governor of Massachusetts in a career that spanned five decades. (Courtesy the Sports Museum.)

SONJA HENIE. Olympic figure skating champion Sonja Henie was a frequent Boston Garden performer. On the night of January 27, 1937, she entertained between periods of a Boston Olympics–Montreal Canadiens exhibition game. With three Olympic gold medals and 10 successive world championships, Henie was a major draw. (Courtesy the Sports Museum.)

JACK SHARKEY. Not only did world heavyweight boxing champion Jack Sharkey own one of the most popular restaurants near Boston Garden (Sharkey's on Canal Street), but he also fought at the Garden on several occasions, including three of the last four fights of his career. He was the only heavyweight champion ever to fight both Jack Dempsey and Joe Louis. After winning his heavyweight crown against Germany's Max Schmeling on June 21, 1932, he would lose his title belt to Italian Primo Carnera a year later on June 29, 1933. (Courtesy the Sports Museum.)

A BOSTON GARDEN ADVERTISEMENT, 1935. Although the claim that the Boston Garden is
"absolutely fireproof and does not contain a single piece of lumber" may be an exaggeration, the
Garden was Boston's premier venue. By 1935, it had played host not only to sporting events,
such as boxing, wrestling, hockey, and track, but also to the circus, rodeos, concerts, trade
shows, and political and religious meetings. (Courtesy the Sports Museum.)

Three

THE 1940S

GENE AUTRY'S WORLD'S CHAMPIONSHIP RODEO. Gene Autry, the riding, roping, and singing cowboy of radio and the silver screen, was one of the most popular and successful celebrities of his day. From November 1 to 11, 1940, he brought his World's Championship Rodeo to the Garden. (Courtesy the New Boston Garden Corporation.)

THE WINTER SPORTS EXPOSITION AND SKI SHOW. Winter sports fans could come to the 1939–1940 Winter Sports Exposition and Ski Show and be treated to such events as the Ice Vanities of 1940; Pierre Benoit, the Canadian juvenile sensation; Roberts and Farley, the eccentric pair; and Dench and Stewart, "Strictly Olympic Style." There were demonstrations of ski jumping, ice-skating, and lessons in downhill skiing. An indoor ski jump dominated the event. (Courtesy the Sports Museum.)

A HOME SHOW. "This house was built in 4 days by Maurice A. Dunlavy, Contractor, 12 Gardner Path, Brookline," boasts the sign in front of this complete home on the floor at the Boston Garden. The postwar boom created a housing shortage, so prefabricated and pattern homes were springing up all over America. Also shown were cars and such housewares as carpets, furniture, and iceboxes. (Courtesy the Sports Museum.)

"THE CARNIVAL OF SPORTS" ON **WHDH.** In the days before television, people relied on radio broadcasters such as Frank Ryan and Leo Egan to bring them the games at home. Longtime Bruins television broadcaster Fred Cusick began his career in radio. (Courtesy the Sports Museum.)

THE BOSTON OLYMPICS. The Boston Olympics were one of the minor-league teams that called the Boston Garden home, along with the Tigers, Cubs, and Braves. In the days of the six-team NHL, there were not enough jobs for all of the talented players, so in addition to serving as development leagues, the minors provided careers for many. In some instances, long established minor-leaguers were reluctant to move up to the big leagues. One player on this squad who went on to a stellar NHL career was Fernie Flaman (second from right, front row). (Courtesy the Sports Museum.)

DOING THE GOOD WORK. In addition to religious rallies by such big names as Aimee Semple McPherson and Billy Graham, the Garden saw shows devoted to the missionary work of such organizations as the Bon Secours Sisters and the Holy Cross Fathers. In addition to raising awareness and funds, such presentations served as a recruiting opportunity for religious orders. (Courtesy the Sports Museum.)

FRANK FALLON. Boston Garden public address announcer Frank Fallon was also one of New England's most famous radio personalities. (Courtesy the Sports Museum.)

THE ICE CAPADES. As a result of Walter Brown's astute management skills, the Ice Capades always secured the best dates at the Boston Garden. (Courtesy the Sports Museum.)

How are YOU getting home tonight?

You who are going by train have nothing to worry about —no broken springs from holes in the road; no parking lot expense; no tough driving against fog, rain or glaring headlights; no traffic to buck.

You who came in by automobile tonight—try the train next time. Whether to the Garden, the theatre, the ball game or any other evening event in town the train is convenient, fast, and you ride relaxed and comfortable.

**Enjoy the _Whole_ Evening
TRAVEL BY TRAIN**

BOSTON and MAINE
RAILROAD
"MINUTE MAN SERVICE"

A BOSTON & MAINE RAILROAD ADVERTISEMENT. Having a train station in the arena was an advantage for those attending events who did not own cars or did not want to face Boston traffic. For a fare "far cheaper than police tags," passengers could come from as far away as Portland, Maine. The Massachusetts Transit Authority (now MBTA) was another option, with the elevated train stopping right in front of the building on Causeway Street. (Courtesy the Sports Museum.)

We Respectfully Solicit Your Patronage

ICE CREAM .15
SODA .10
CANDY .10
PEANUTS .10
FRANKS .15
POP CORN .15
BEER and ALE .25

BOSTON GARDEN ARENA CORP.
CONCESSION DEPT.

CONCESSIONS. The fare was basic in the 1940s, with staples such as hot dogs and popcorn driving revenue. In later years, Boston Garden pizza was known as the best arena pizza in America. (Courtesy the Sports Museum.)

STEVE "CRUSHER" CASEY. At the height of the Great Depression, Steve "Crusher" Casey arrived in Boston from Ireland in 1936 with brothers Jim and Tom and soon achieved celebrity as one of the greatest wrestlers (and Boston Garden performers) of his generation. Known as the "Irish Adonis," Casey entertained crowds with his famous Kerry Crush and Killarney Flip holds. Casey is shown in his U.S. Army uniform during World War II. (Courtesy the Sports Museum.)

"DOGGIE" JULIAN. Alvin "Doggie" Julian coached the Celtics during the transitional years from BAA to National Basketball Association (NBA) rules. A college coach before he arrived in Boston, Julian led the Holy Cross Crusaders to a National Collegiate Athletic Association (NCAA) championship in 1947. Taking over as coach of the Celtics in 1948, Julian's career was less than stellar (47-81). Released by Walter Brown after two years behind the bench, Julian returned to college coaching, where he enjoyed success in the 1950s and 1960s. His service with the National Association of Basketball Coaches (NABC) and his 32-year coaching career led to his election to the Basketball Hall of Fame in 1967. (John C. Ferguson photograph, courtesy the Sports Museum.)

BOB COUSY AT HOLY CROSS. Although a star at Holy Cross, new Celtics coach Red Auerbach wanted no part of the unproven local Bob Cousy. He was drafted instead by the Tri-Cities Hawks. The Celtics had another chance at Cousy when his rights were traded to Chicago, but again they passed. When the Stags folded, the rights to the top three players were divided by a draw from a hat and the Celtics, who picked last, ended up with Cousy. The "Houdini of the Hardwood" went on to be one of the best players in NBA history, leading the Celtics to championships in 1957, 1959, 1960, 1961, 1962, and 1963. He came out of retirement in 1969–1970 to play seven games as player-coach in Cincinnati. Cousy was elected to the Basketball Hall of Fame in 1970. (Courtesy the Sports Museum.)

CHUCK CONNORS. A superb two-sport athlete, Chuck Connors played for the Celtics as well as the Cubs and Dodgers before going on to fame on *The Rifleman* television show during the 1950s and 1960s. His breaking of a backboard caused a major delay in the playing of the first Celtics home game at Boston Arena in November 1946. (Courtesy the Sports Museum.)

THE ROLLER DERBY. Extreme sports are nothing new to Boston Garden fans. Roller Derby was played on an oval track with no ball, net, or goal. It consisted of two teams of five players, plus substitutes. Roller Derby players were just as often women as men. The game was divided into two halves, with four 15-minute periods making up a half. The object of the game was to lap the opposition, or to completely circle the opposing team after pulling away from the pack, or the rest of the field. This pulling away process was called a jam. Points were scored as a result of these jams, one point when a skater lapped one member of the opposition, two when a skater passed three members, and five when the entire five members of the enemy had been lapped. All this had to be accomplished in a two-minute time frame. The real attraction of the game was the blocking, body checking, and rough housing. Roller Derby was not a sport for the faint of heart. (Courtesy the Sports Museum.)

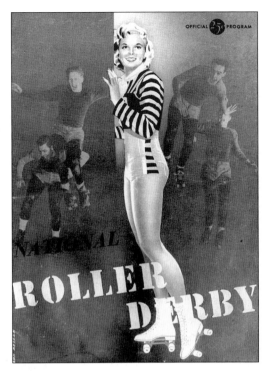

THE BOSTON GARDEN PROGRAM. The Bruins faced the Toronto Maple Leafs in Stanley Cup action on the night of April 1, 1948. Toronto would beat the Bruins in five games and go on to sweep Detroit in the finals, capturing their second cup in a row. In the postwar, pre-expansion era, the NHL was dominated by Montreal, Toronto, and Detroit. From the time the Bruins won the cup in 1941 until they recaptured it in 1970, Toronto won 10 times, Detroit 5, and Montreal 12. This sweep was interrupted only once in those years, when the Chicago Blackhawks beat Detroit to win in 1961. (Courtesy the Sports Museum.)

THE BRUINS ON THE BENCH, 1948. This unusual view of the Bruins bench during a December 1948 game against the Montreal Canadiens shows how close Garden fans sat to the action. The coach is the recently retired longtime Bruins star Dit Clapper. Clapper, the NHL's first 20-year player (all with the Bruins), coached the team, first as player-coach and then behind the bench,

from 1945 to 1949. The players seen here are, from left to right, Ed Kryzanowski, Ed Harrison, Ed Sandford, Fernie Flaman, Grant Warwick, Johnny Crawford, Pete Babando, and Jim Peters. (Boston Herald photograph, courtesy the Sports Museum.)

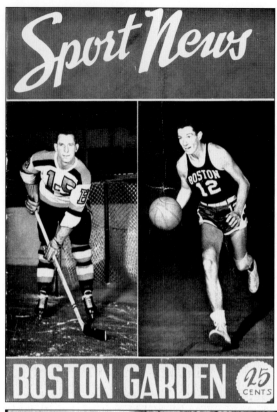

A Boston Garden Program, 1947–1948. This 32-page program, featuring Bruins captain Milt Schmidt and Celtics star Art Spector on the cover, sold for a price of 25¢. For that price, the customer got a scorecard with the lineup of that night's Bruins–Maple Leafs game, several articles on the Bruins, Celtics, college basketball, schoolboy tournaments, and the minor-league Boston Olympics, as well as advertisements for Hood ice cream, Bulova watches, the Boston & Maine Railroad's snow trains, Old Gold cigarettes, Narragansett Lager, Jordan Marsh, LaTouraine Coffee, and the Hotel Manger. (Courtesy the Sports Museum.)

Winston Churchill at the Boston Garden. On March 31, 1949, Winston Churchill addressed the Massachusetts Institute of Technology Mid-Century Convocation. In his speech, Churchill declared, among other things, that the atomic bomb had saved Europe. (Courtesy the New Boston Garden Corporation.)

Four

THE 1950S

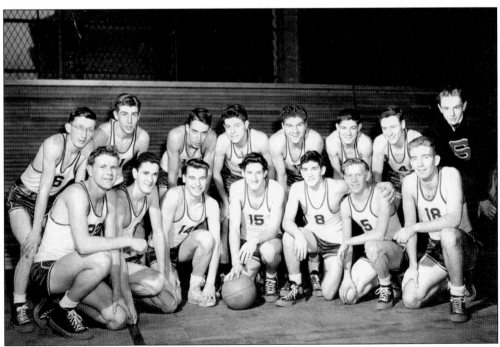

SOMERVILLE HIGH SCHOOL BASKETBALL TEAM. Led by Ronnie Perry, John Nunziato, and Stump Macdonald, the Somerville High School basketball team of 1950 marched to the Boston Garden led by a band and thousands of fans. Following their tournament victory, fans tore up Boston phone books and showered the Boston Garden with homemade confetti. In time, they played doubleheaders in tandem with the Boston Celtics. (Courtesy the Sports Museum.)

ROCKY MARCIANO. On August 27, 1951, Brockton native Rocky Marciano made his only Boston Garden appearance, defeating Fred Breshore with a fourth-round knockout. (Courtesy the Sports Museum.)

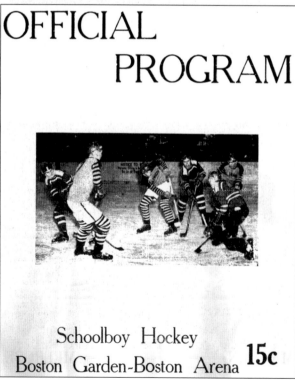

OFFICIAL

PROGRAM

Schoolboy Hockey
Boston Garden-Boston Arena **15c**

SCHOOLBOY HOCKEY PROGRAM, C. 1951. Schoolboy hockey was a staple of the Boston Garden and Boston Arena. Associations such as the Bay State League, Eastern Massachusetts League, and the Greater Boston League played there. Although a second-tier facility after the Garden was built, Boston Arena still saw much use by high school, collegiate semiprofessional, minor professional, and amateur hockey teams over the years. Currently owned by Northeastern University, it is known as Matthews Arena. (Courtesy the Sports Museum.)

SCHMIDT-DUMART NIGHT, MARCH 18, 1952. On the night of March 18, 1952, fans saw the Kraut Line play together one last time. Milt Schmidt, Woody Dumart, and Bobby Bauer made up one of the most famous lines in hockey in the 1930s and 1940s. The three Kitchener, Ontario natives had played together, roomed together, and even went off to war together until Bobby Bauer's retirement at age 32 in 1947. When the Bruins honored Schmidt and Dumart (still playing for the team) with a night in 1952, it was decided to let Bauer come out of retirement to play one last game. A successful sporting goods manufacturer, Bauer had kept his skating legs in shape as the player-coach of the Waterloo-Kitchener Dutchmen, a senior amateur team. After ceremonies and presentations, it was like old times as the Krauts faced off against the Chicago Blackhawks. Although his "comeback" lasted only one game, it gave fans a chance to see the magic once again. (Courtesy the Sports Museum.)

FRANK SINATRA AT THE BOSTON GARDEN. On June 17, 1952, Frank Sinatra hosted a "Bands for Israel" night. (Courtesy the Boston Herald.)

THE RODEO PARADE. The Old West comes to Boston as rodeo performers parade down Tremont Street in the 1950s. A modern spectator standing on the same spot would easily

recognize the area, especially Boston Common, the Park Street subway station, and Park Street Church. (Courtesy the Sports Museum.)

DURFEE VERSUS MISSION, C. 1953.
Boston's tiny Mission High School was one of the great Tech Tournament Cinderella stories as they beat much larger schools. In this photograph, Tom Clarke of Mission is shown driving for a basket against Paul Bogan of Fall River's Durfee High School. (Courtesy Richard A. Johnson.)

EISENHOWER PRESIDENTIAL RALLY, NOVEMBER 3, 1952. Presidential candidate Dwight D. Eisenhower lectures the Boston Garden crowd against the scourge of "Godless Communism." Along with running mate Richard Nixon, the popular former general would defeat Democrat Adlai Stevenson to take the White House the next day. He carried 39 states with 34 million popular votes, the most by a presidential candidate up to that time. (Courtesy the New Boston Garden Corporation.)

TOMMY COLLINS VERSUS WILLIE PEP, c. 1952. This featherweight bout between Boston's Tommy Collins and Willie Pep was won by Collins in a knockout. Boxing was long a staple of the Garden, attracting the biggest names in every weight class. (Courtesy the Sports Museum.)

TONY DEMARCO. Victorious Tony Demarco is hoisted into the air by his trainer, Sammy Fuller. Born Leonardo Liotta in Boston's North End, Tony DeMarco adopted the name of an older local boy in order to secure permission to box. His career reached its zenith on April 1, 1955, as the 23-year-old welterweight won the world welterweight championship in the Boston Garden in a 14-round knockout over Johnny Saxton. DeMarco would defend and lose his title against Carmen Basilio on June 10, 1955. (Associated Press photograph, courtesy the Sports Museum.)

TOM HEINSOHN AT GAME SEVEN OF THE 1957 FINALS. Tom Heinsohn, despondent over fouling out of the game, covers his head with his warmup jacket. Although he fouled out, his 36-point performance was a key part of the Celtics victory. (Courtesy the Sports Museum.)

THE 1957–1958 BOSTON CELTICS. Although they lost in the finals to the St. Louis Hawks, this team formed the core of the Celtics championship teams of the 1950s and early 1960s. Seen here are, from left to right, Frank Ramsay, Arnie Risen, Togo Palazzi, Jim Loscutoff, Dick Hemric, Tom Heinsohn, Andy Philip, Sam Jones, Bill Russell, Bill Sharman, Bob Cousy, and Red Auerbach. (Courtesy the Sports Museum.)

A STEEL CAGE WRESTLING MATCH, C. 1959. It took a steel cage, or more accurately, a chain-link fence, in the ring to contain these wrestlers. (Courtesy the Sports Museum.)

THE TECH TOURNAMENT BY GENE MACK. The Eastern, or Tech, Basketball Tournament was one of the most popular annual events at the Garden. It was especially a favorite of the great *Boston Globe* sports cartoonist Gene Mack. Born Eugene McGillicuddy and a distant relative of baseball's Connie Mack, the North Cambridge native was a master of cartoon storytelling. Readers could get the whole story of the games through the tiny, yet animated, figures. (Courtesy the Sports Museum.)

TENLEY ALBRIGHT, C. 1956. Brookline native Tenley Albright used figure skating to overcome childhood polio. She won a silver medal in Oslo (1952) and a gold medal in Cortina d'Ampezzo (1956). Albright graduated from Harvard University and Harvard Medical School and went on to become an orthopedic surgeon. (Courtesy the Sports Museum.)

A BOSTON & MAINE RAILROAD ADVERTISEMENT. Why drive when the train stops right in North Station? The Boston & Maine Railroad provided a convenient alternative to driving and parking in Boston. (Courtesy the Sports Museum.)

WALTER BROWN AND CELTICS PLAYERS. Shown here in the cozy confines of their Boston Garden locker room, team owner Walter Brown chats with such stars as Bob Cousy (with hat), Jim Loscutoff (in jacket), and Bill Sharman (with envelope). (Courtesy the Sports Museum.)

THE BRUINS VERSUS DETROIT, CHRISTMAS 1957. They still played on Christmas night back in the 1950s. Thanks to the players union, the NHL gets a Christmas break to allow players and officials to spend time with their families. This $2.50 ticket from December 25, 1957, would get you a promenade seat. (Courtesy the Sports Museum.)

THE 1957 NBA FINALS.
In 1957, the Celtics
defeated the St. Louis
Hawks to take their first
NBA championship. Bill
Russell is seen going up
against Hawks star Bob
Petit. (Courtesy the
Sports Museum.)

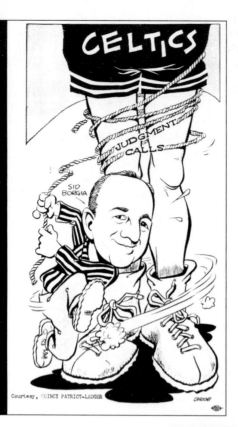

THE CELTICS JUNIOR BOOSTER CLUB NEWS, c. 1955. Young Celtics fans had a forum in this fan-club publication. In addition to articles, it contained schedules, statistics, basketball tips, and more. It was produced for Celtics fans by the team and served as a way for the team to communicate with its most ardent supporters. Featured on the cover of this January 1955 issue was a cartoon of longtime officiating nemesis Sid Borgia by *Quincy Patriot Ledger* cartoonist Bill Robertson. (Courtesy the Sports Museum.)

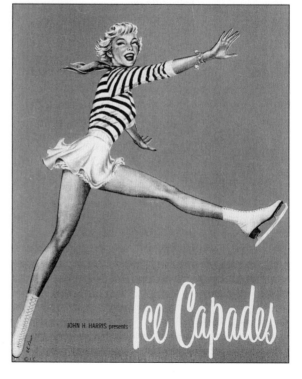

THE ICE CAPADES. The Ice Capades, the Ice Follies, and other skating shows were a popular attraction at the Garden. Colorful programs featuring comely skaters gave patrons a lineup that included exhibition skating, ice dancing, humor, and spectacle. (Courtesy the Sports Museum.)

A BOSTON GARDEN EVENTS SCHEDULE. Boston Garden was a busy place in the 1950s. This event schedule from a 1957–1958 season Boston Garden sports-news program shows something happening almost every day of February into early March. In addition to the Bruins and Celtics, there were the immensely popular Ice Follies, the Beanpot, the Silver Skates Derby, and the Eastern Massachusetts interscholastic basketball trials. Note that before the Celtics game against the Syracuse Nationals on February 12, 1958, Goose Tatum's Harlem Stars faced off against the New York Olympians. (Courtesy the Sports Museum.)

BOSTON GARDEN
SPORT-NEWS

SEASON OF 1957-1958   VOL. XXX — NO. 10

Official Publication of Boston Garden-Arena Corporation
WALTER A. BROWN, President   LES STOUT, Editor

BOSTON GARDEN EVENTS

Thu.	Feb. 6	N.H.L. Hockey—BRUINS vs Chicago Black Hawks—8 P.M.
Fri.	Feb. 7	N.B.A. Basketball—CELTICS vs Minneapolis Lakers—9:15 P.M.
		New York vs Syracuse—7:15 P.M.
Sun.	Feb. 9	(Aft.) Silver Skates Derby—1 P.M.
		(Eve.) N.H.L. Hockey—BRUINS vs Toronto Maple Leafs—7:30 P.M.
Mon.	Feb. 10	Intercollegiate Hockey—Beanpot Tournament—7 P.M.
		Northeastern, Harvard, Boston College, Boston University.
Wed.	Feb. 12	N.B.A. Basketball—CELTICS vs Syracuse Nationals—9 P.M.
		Goose Tatum's Harlem Stars vs N.Y. Olympians—7:15 P.M.
Thu.	Feb. 13	N.H.L. Hockey—BRUINS vs Detroit Red Wings—8 P.M.
Fri.	Feb. 14	N.B.A. Basketball—CELTICS vs Detroit Pistons—8 P.M.
Sat.	Feb. 15	(Aft.) N.H.L. Hockey—BRUINS vs Montreal Canadiens—2 P.M.
Sun.	Feb. 16	(Aft.) N.B.A.—Basketball—CELTICS vs New York Knicks—2:30 P.M.
Tue.	Feb. 18	ICE FOLLIES of 1958—8 P.M.
Wed.	Feb. 19	ICE FOLLIES of 1958—2:30 & 8 P.M.
Thu.	Feb. 20	ICE FOLLIES of 1958—8 P.M.
Fri.	Feb. 21	ICE FOLLIES of 1958—8 P.M.
Sat.	Feb. 22	ICE FOLLIES of 1958—1:00, 5.00 & 9 P.M.
Sun.	Feb. 23	ICE FOLLIES of 1958—1:30 & 5:30 P.M.
Mon.	Feb. 24	Eastern Mass. Interscholastic Basketball Trials
Tue.	Feb. 25	Eastern Mass. Interscholastic Basketball Trials
Wed.	Feb. 26	ICE FOLLIES of 1958—2:30 & 8 P.M.
Thu.	Feb. 27	ICE FOLLIES of 1958—8 P.M.
Fri.	Feb. 28	ICE FOLLIES of 1958—8 P.M.
Sat.	Mar. 1	ICE FOLLIES of 1958—1, 5 & 9 P.M.
Sun.	Mar. 2	ICE FOLLIES of 1958—1:30 & 5:30 P.M.
Wed.	Mar. 5	N.B.A. Basketball—CELTICS vs. St. Louis Hawks—9:15 P.M.
		Harlem Magicians

Official Program

67th Annual

B.A.A.
INDOOR GAMES

JAN. 28
1956

50¢

BOSTON GARDEN

THE BAA GAMES TRACK PROGRAM. The old wooden track of the Boston Garden was hauled out twice a year for the BAA and Knights of Columbus indoor track meets. The meets began shortly after lunch with schoolboy events and concluded nearly 12 hours later with the open meet. (Courtesy the Sports Museum.)

59

A VIEW OF WALTER BROWN IN HIS OFFICE. Not only was Walter Brown the founder and guiding light of the Boston Celtics, but he was the most well-respected and successful owner in the history of both the NBA and Boston sports history. Brown made great personal and

financial sacrifices to keep the franchise alive and build the foundation of basketball's greatest dynasty. (Courtesy the Sports Museum.)

A Basketball Luncheon on the Garden Floor. What better place for a basketball luncheon than on the parquet? While the famous floor was covered with a protective surface, diners ate under the baskets in the shadow of the old score clock. (Courtesy the Sports Museum.)

Liberace. Television made him a star, but performing before a live audience was Liberace's first love. On November 12, 1954, "Mr. Showmanship" brought his own brand of classical and kitsch to the Garden in his first big concert. The immensely popular pianist signed autographs until 3:00 a.m. He is shown here at the Garden in the 1970s. (Courtesy the Sports Museum.)

Five

THE 1960s

JOHN F. KENNEDY RALLY, NOVEMBER 1960. On the eve of the 1960 presidential election, native son John Fitzgerald Kennedy made a triumphant return to Boston, holding his last rally at the Boston Garden. An estimated 10,000 people jammed the street while 20,000 made it inside to listen to Kennedy's speech. This became the largest crowd ever inside the Boston Garden. Just 14 years earlier, Kennedy had plotted his political future while attending hockey games in the arena with his friend and confidante Dave Powers. (Courtesy the New Boston Garden Corporation.)

Bob (left) and Bill Cleary (wearing his Olympic uniform) are shown here with their parents. The brothers were two of the best players to come out of Boston. Both graduates of Harvard, they played on the 1960 gold medal–winning Olympic team, with Bill scoring the game-winning goal against the Soviet Union. Bill Cleary went on to coach and serve as athletic director at Harvard. As coach, he led the Crimson to the 1989 NCAA championship. The elder Cleary was a referee for many years in the Boston area. (Courtesy the Sports Museum.)

MILT SCHMIDT COACHES THE BRUINS, 1965. A member of the Kraut Line with Woody Dumart and Bobby Bauer, Schmidt played from 1936 to 1955, with time off for military service in World War II. He played on two Stanley Cup teams (1939 and 1941) and won the Dufresne Trophy in 1942 (along with Bauer and Dumart), 1947, 1950, and 1951. He coached the Bruins from 1954 to 1961 and again from 1962 to 1966. As the general manager from 1967 to 1972, he engineered the trade that brought Phil Esposito, Ken Hodge, and Fred Stanfield to Boston. He was elected to the Hockey Hall of Fame in 1961. (Boston Herald photograph.)

COONEY WEILAND AND HARVARD
CAPTAIN C. STEWART FORBES, C. 1961.
Weiland, along with his Minneapolis Miller
teammate Tiny Thompson, joined the Bruins
in 1928 and helped lead Boston to their first
Stanley Cup. Weiland was also member of
the 1939 Stanley Cup champions and
coached Boston to another cup in 1941. He
later went on to coach at Harvard for 21
seasons, winning 315 games. (Courtesy the
Sports Museum.)

HIGH JUMPER JOHN THOMAS. Not only was Cambridge native and Boston University alumnus
John Thomas a bronze and silver medalist in the high jump at the 1960 and 1964 Olympics,
but he also dazzled fans with his indoor jumps. On February 1, 1960, the Boston University
freshman made a dramatic return from a foot injury with a world-record jump of seven feet, one
and a half inches. (Courtesy John Thomas.)

RODEO HORSES STABLED IN THE GARDEN. When the rodeo or circus came to town, the animals would be kept in the Garden. Coming up the elephant ramp out back, creatures ranging from bears to zebras would make their home in the broad access or storage areas just off the event floor. In the tradition of the old circus parade, animals appearing at the FleetCenter

are often kept in cages in the old Boston Garden lot (the area out front where the Garden once stood) to attract and entertain the passing crowds. (Jerry Buckley photograph, courtesy the Sports Museum.)

WILLIE O'REE. Although his NHL career consisted of only 45 games over parts of two seasons (1957–1958 and 1960–1961), Willie O'Ree will always be remembered as the first black player in the NHL, being called up in January 1958. He spent most of his career in the minors, retiring in 1980. (Al Ruelle photograph, courtesy the Sports Museum.)

JUDY GARLAND. Legendary performer Judy Garland dazzled the sold-out crowd on October 27, 1961. Scalpers were reportedly getting as much as $9 a ticket! (Courtesy the New Boston Garden Corporation.)

BOB COUSY DAY

BOSTON CELTICS

NATIONAL BASKETBALL ASSOCIATION

BOB COUSY

FEX

BOSTON GARDEN, MARCH 17, 1963   SOUVENIR PROGRAM *50¢*

THE BOB COUSY DAY PROGRAM. On St. Patrick's Day 1963, Bob Cousy was honored for his dozen seasons with the Celtics. As Cousy paused to wipe away tears during an emotional thank-you speech, a leather-lung fan shouted the unforgettable "We love ya Cooz" to the hushed crowd. (Courtesy Richard A. Johnson.)

69

RIP VALENTI. The sage of Canal Street, boxing promoter Rip Valenti, was the dean of sports promoters in Boston, having worked with them all from Joe Louis to Muhammad Ali. (Angela Kalovetzos photograph, courtesy the Sports Museum.)

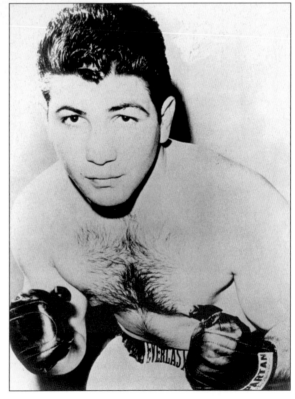

JOE DENUCCI. Although Joe DeNucci never captured a world title as a light-heavyweight boxer, he will always have the distinction of having fought more professional bouts than any boxer in Boston Garden history. The Newton native became a title contender over his decade-long career, which ended in 1968. Following his boxing career, he made the transition to local and state politics, where he currently serves the Commonwealth as state auditor. (Courtesy the Sports Museum.)

70

BILL RUSSELL AND WILT CHAMBERLAIN. It was a clash of the Titans when these two met on the court. The two best players and greatest rivals of their generation, Russell racked up championships while Chamberlain amassed scoring titles. Although friends off the court, a match up between the Celtics and the Sixers (and later the Lakers) promised an unrivaled display of basketball competition. (Dick Raphael photograph.)

WESTON ADAMS SR. Charles F. Adams was the original owner of the Bruins and helped bring the team three Stanley Cup championships. After his graduation from Harvard, his son Weston became a director of the team. He learned the business by serving in several positions, including president of the minor-league Boston Tigers. He took over as Bruins president in 1936 and, except for service in World War II, was associated with the Bruins and Boston Garden until his death in 1973. (Courtesy the Sports Museum.)

JOHN BUCYK. "The Chief" played 23 seasons, 21 with Boston, and was the de facto captain on two Stanley Cup teams (1970 and 1972). A two-time Lady Byng Trophy winner (1971 and 1974), Bucyk also won the Lester Patrick Trophy (1977) and the Dufresne Trophy (1963 and 1966). He retired in 1978 and was elected to the Hockey Hall of Fame in 1981. Bucyk remains active in Bruins alumni events. (Al Ruelle photograph, courtesy the Hockey Hall of Fame.)

72

PAUL PENDER. Brookline native Paul Pender joined an exclusive club of local boxers on January 22, 1960, when he won the world middleweight boxing title against the immortal Sugar Ray Robinson at Boston Garden. Pender would go on to defend his title against Robinson on June 10, 1960, and would again defeat the former champion in a 15-round decision. In his last four bouts, Pender would successfully defend his title twice against Terry Downes and Carmen Basilio before losing the title to Downes and regaining it on April 7, 1962. Pender retired from boxing in 1963. (Courtesy the Sports Museum.)

PAUL PENDER AND TERRY DOWNES, APRIL 7, 1962. A not-quite-full house watches Paul Pender

defeat Terry Downes in a middleweight championship bout. (Courtesy the Sports Museum.)

THE BEATLES PLAY BOSTON GARDEN. On September 12, 1964, the British Invasion hit Boston when the Beatles played the Garden. More than 200 policemen were required to keep order as the Fab Four wowed the crowd in what would be their only Boston Garden appearance. (Courtesy the New Boston Garden Corporation.)

A CARPET SALE AT THE BOSTON GARDEN, MAY 1967. The Garden was home to more than sporting events, concerts, and rallies. For three days in 1967, J.C. Best held a carpet sale on the floor of the arena. No shortage of carpets or signage greeted shoppers as they looked over acres of rugs. Note the old score clock with the "Boston Garden" framing the analog clock. (Courtesy the Sports Museum.)

EDDIE SHORE TAKES THE ICE ONCE AGAIN. Still formidable at the age of 64, Eddie Shore waves to the crowd before an old-timers game in 1967. Crowded into the old arena to see the game were 11,093 fans. (Boston Herald photograph, courtesy the Sports Museum.)

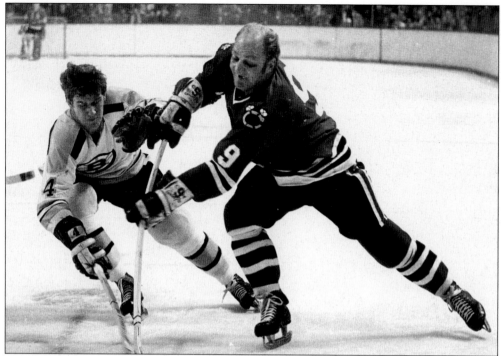

BOBBY ORR CHALLENGES BOBBY HULL. To Boston fans, Bobby Orr was in a league by himself. The winner of eight Norris Trophies for best defenseman, three times the league MVP, twice its leading scorer, twice awarded the Conn Smythe Trophy as playoff MVP, as well as the rookie of the year in 1967, Orr revolutionized the defenseman's role. Whether rushing end to end or playing keep away from an entire opposing team, Orr electrified the NHL for 12 seasons. (Al Ruelle photograph, courtesy the Sports Museum.)

A VIEW FROM THE BALCONY. The home of the Gallery Gods, cheap seats, and kids who snuck in via the fire escape, the balcony of the Garden offered a bird's-eye view of the action. (Pam Schuyler photograph, courtesy the Sports Museum.)

RED AUERBACH, 1966. Coach Red Auerbach clenches his fist and clutches his trademark rolled-up program as he watches his team lose to the Lakers on Red Auerbach Day, February 13, 1966. Despite the festive occasion, the always combative Auerbach was hit with a technical foul in the game. Auerbach has the distinction of being the only coach to be tossed out of an all-star game and an old-timers game. "They keep score, I like to win," he once explained. (Courtesy the Sports Museum.)

THE BOSTON UNIVERSITY TERRIERS CELEBRATE THEIR 1966 BEANPOT TRIUMPH. In this view, coach Jack Kelley (in hat) accepts the trophy from Boston Garden general manager Eddie Powers. Standing directly behind Kelley and Powers is a young Jack Parker, who later forged a

career as one of the greatest college hockey coaches of all time and was the undisputed king of the Beanpot. (Courtesy the Sports Museum.)

Fourteenth Annual

BEANPOT
INTERCOLLEGIATE HOCKEY
TOURNAMENT

**BOSTON
COLLEGE**

**BOSTON
UNIVERSITY**

**HARVARD
UNIVERSITY**

**NORTHEASTERN
UNIVERSITY**

1966

FEBRUARY 7 and FEBRUARY 14
• BOSTON GARDEN •

PROGRAM *25¢*

THE BEANPOT. The 1966 Beanpot marked the first of a three-cup run for the Boston University Terriers. In subsequent years, they have dominated the tournament. (Courtesy the Sports Museum.)

Six
THE 1970S

BOBBY ORR DRINKS FROM THE
STANLEY CUP. The Stanley Cup win
was front-page news all across New
England. No one made it possible more
than Bobby Orr. Orr won the Calder
Trophy as rookie of the year in 1966, the
Norris Trophy as best defenseman from
1967–1968 through 1974–1975, the Art
Ross Trophy as leading scorer in
1974–1975, the Hart Trophy as MVP
from 1969–1970 through 1971–1972,
and the Conn Smythe Trophy as playoff
MVP in 1969–1970 and 1971–1972. He
won the Dufresne Trophy in 1967, 1970,
1972, 1974 (co-winner), and 1975. Orr
played on two Stanley Cup teams (1970
and 1972) and was an eight-time first
team all-star. Considered by most to be
the greatest player in NHL history, he
was elected to the Hockey Hall of Fame
in 1979. The highlight of this edition of
the Boston *Record-American* was a
centerfold of Ray Lussier's photograph of
Orr's game-winning goal. (Courtesy the
Sports Museum.)

Bobby Orr Wins the Stanley Cup. Bruins fans know where they were at the moment Bobby Orr scored in overtime on the afternoon of May 10, 1970, as the Bruins swept the St. Louis Blues for their first Stanley Cup in 29 years. This image of Orr being upended by Noel

Picard after having just beaten goalie Glenn Hall is one of the most enduring photographs of Boston sports history. (Ray Lussier photograph, courtesy the Boston Herald.)

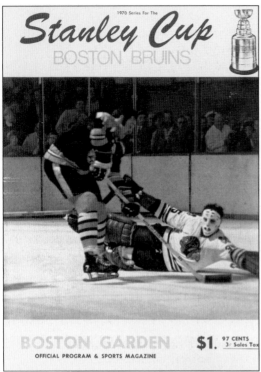

THE 1970 STANLEY CUP PROGRAM.
Bruins star Phil Esposito is shown facing his brother, Chicago rookie Tony Esposito (Tony had played briefly for the Montreal Canadiens but was still considered a rookie). He won the Calder Trophy as rookie of the year as well as the Vezina Trophy as top goaltender. None of this helped the Blackhawks. Bobby Orr had hit his full stride with a dazzling season, becoming the first defenseman to lead the league in scoring. The Bruins also gelled as a team behind Orr and Esposito with career performances by such veterans as John Bucyk, Ed Westfall, Ken Hodge, and John McKenzie, as well as the stellar goaltending of Gerry Cheevers. After defeating the Rangers in six games, the Bruins swept the Blackhawks to advance to the finals against St. Louis. The Blues were defeated by the Bruins in four games, climaxing with Orr's now famous overtime goal. (Courtesy the Sports Museum.)

A STANLEY CUP CELEBRATION, 1970. On May 10, 1970, Bobby Orr scored the winning goal to end the Bruins 29-year Stanley Cup drought. Shown in the locker room are, from left to right, Milt Schmidt, general manager and veteran of the last cup win in 1941; Tom Johnson, assistant general manager; Bobby Orr; and Harry Sinden, coach. (Al Ruelle photograph, courtesy the Sports Museum.)

THE 1971 ALL-STAR GAME PROGRAM. In the first and only NHL all-star game held at the Boston Garden, the Eastern All Stars were defeated 2-1 in an atypical defensive battle. Bobby Orr, Ed Westfall, Ken Hodge, Phil Esposito, and Dallas Smith, along with coach Harry Sinden, John Bucyk, and Johnny McKenzie (who did not play due to injuries) were chosen to represent the Stanley Cup champion Bruins at the game. (Courtesy the Sports Museum.)

ELVIS PRESLEY. On November 10, 1971, the King made his only appearance at the Boston Garden. Although by this time he had made the transition from rebel leather to Vegas glitz, Elvis still put on an exhibition of rock-and-roll that had the audience dancing in the aisles. (Courtesy the New Boston Garden Corporation.)

The 1971–1972 Boston University Hockey Team. The 1971–1972 Terrier hockey team, led by coach Jack Kelley, defeated Cornell University at the Garden and took their first

national championship. (Courtesy the Sports Museum.)

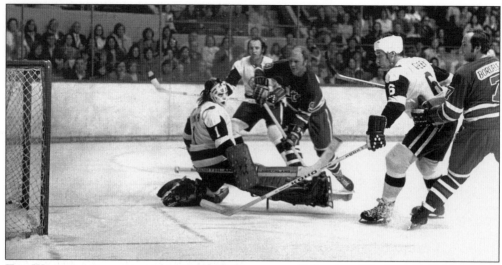

THE WHALERS VERSUS THE JETS. Bobby Hull scores on Al Smith as Whaler captain Ted Green looks on. With a combination of NHL castoffs, minor-leaguers, and a handful of stars, the World Hockey Association (WHA) set out to threaten the NHL's exclusive dominance of professional hockey. Toronto's Bernie Parent was the first NHL star signed, but it was the astonishing 10-year, $2.75 million contract given to Blackhawks star Bobby Hull that opened the floodgate of NHL defections. Soon, major players such as J.C. Tremblay of Montreal, Paul Henderson of Toronto, and Gerry Cheevers, Johnnie McKenzie, and Ted Green of Boston were changing leagues. Derek Sanderson signed a 10-year contract with the Philadelphia Blazers worth a reported $2.35 million in August 1972, but after only eight games and six points, his contract was bought out, and he was back in black and gold by January. (Courtesy the Sports Museum.)

AVCO WORLD CUP CELEBRATION. Former Bruins Tommy "Bomber" Williams and Ted Green kiss the Avco World Cup, symbolic of the WHA championship, at the Boston Garden in 1973. The upstart league, having raided the NHL for players, had an uneasy coexistence as Garden tenants until the Whalers departed for Hartford in January 1975. The badly decimated league folded in 1979, and the Edmonton Oilers, Winnipeg Jets, Quebec Nordiques, and New England Whalers were absorbed by the NHL as expansion teams. (Courtesy the Sports Museum.)

90

OLGA KORBUT. Olga Korbut led a team of Soviet gymnasts to the Boston Garden for an exhibition series in 1974. (Courtesy the Sports Museum.)

BILLIE JEAN KING. Not only was Billie Jean King one of the greatest players in tennis history, but she also helped found the Virginia Slims Women's Tennis Tour, the Women's Tennis Association, and the Women's Sports Foundation. She is shown at the Boston Garden during a Virginia Slims event. (Courtesy the Sports Museum.)

THE ROLLING STONES, 1975. The Rolling Stones remained loyal Boston Garden performers following their legendary 1972 show. On that night, panic ensued due to their drug bust in Rhode Island that almost forced a cancellation of the show. Because of direct intervention by Boston Mayor Kevin White, the show was allowed to go on at 12:45 a.m., after the Stones were released and rushed north from Rhode Island. (Courtesy the Sports Museum.)

HARRY SINDEN. A premier amateur hockey player, Harry Sinden began in the Bruins organization in 1961 following a silver medal–winning performance with Team Canada in the 1960 Olympics. After a coaching stint in Minneapolis, he became player-coach in Oklahoma City in 1965, leading the club to the Canadian Hockey League championship. He was named Bruins head coach in 1966, the same year that Bobby Orr joined the club. After winning the Stanley Cup in 1970, Sinden left hockey for two years to pursue a business career. Asked to coach Team Canada in 1972, he led the team to victory over the Soviet Union. After the series concluded, he returned to Boston to become the fifth general manager in Bruins history. He is currently the president of the team. Sinden was inducted into the Hockey Hall of Fame in 1983. (Courtesy the Sports Museum.)

DAVE COWENS, C. 1976. Kentucky native "Big Red" Cowens played center like a power forward, with the speed and quickness of a guard, while helping lead the Green to titles in 1974 and 1976. A fiery competitor, he was co-rookie of the year in 1970 and league MVP in 1973. (Courtesy the Sports Museum.)

THE 1976 BOSTON CELTICS WORLD CHAMPIONS AT CITY HALL. This stylish group ruled the basketball world in 1976. Seen here are, from left to right, the following: (front row) Jim Ard, Jerome Anderson, Glenn McDonald, and Kevin Stacom; (back row) Dave Cowens, Paul Silas,

Jo Jo White, John Havlicek, Don Nelson, Charlie Scott, Steve Kuberski, and Tom Boswell. (Courtesy the Sports Museum.)

JOHN HAVLICEK, C. 1973. "Hondo," shown here playing against Bill Bradley and the New York Knicks, played 16 seasons, winning eight world championships. He was all-NBA 11 times and played in 13 all-star games. Havlicek was also a member of the NBA 35th anniversary team and was elected to the Basketball Hall of Fame in 1983. (Frank O'Brien photograph, courtesy the Sports Museum.)

DON CHERRY AND BLUE, C. 1978.
Scrappy, pugnacious, outspoken, and outrageous are words used to describe Don Cherry, the coach who held rein the "Lunch Pail" Bruins of the late 1970s. Taking over behind the bench in 1974, Cherry coached the Bruins until 1979. After retiring from coaching, Cherry became a popular broadcaster-commentator, known for his loud suits and louder opinions. (Courtesy the Sports Museum.)

TERRY O'REILLY, C. 1979. Terry O'Reilly epitomized the "Lunch Pail" Bruins. Arriving in the Orr era in the early 1970s after playing with the minor-league Boston Braves, O'Reilly quickly became a fan favorite. A fighter who never backed down and led by example, "Taz" played his entire career (1971–1985) in black and gold. He wore the captain's C from 1983 to 1985, and coached the club from 1986 to 1989. Shown with O'Reilly are Don Marcotte and Mike Milbury. Born in Brighton and raised in Walpole, Milbury was also a tough competitor who succeeded O'Reilly as coach of the team (1989–1991). (Pamela Schuyler-Cowens photograph.)

LARRY BIRD IN ACTION. Larry Bird played 13 seasons and won three world championships, 1981, 1984, and 1986. He was college player of the year in 1979, NBA rookie of the year and all-rookie team in 1980. A three-time MVP (1984, 1985, and 1986), nine-time first team all-star, all-star MVP in 1982, and NBA finals MVP in 1984 and 1986, Bird was also the Sporting News man of the year in 1986, and AP male athlete of the year in 1986. He played on the 1993 Olympic gold medal–winning Dream Team. (Courtesy the Sports Museum.)

IN BIRD WE TRUST. This novelty $33 bill featured Larry Bird, always money in the bank for the Celtics. A rookie in 1979, Bird would lead the team to championships in 1981, 1984, and 1986. (Larry Bell donation, courtesy the Sports Museum.)

Seven

THE 1980s

TINY ARCHIBALD AND RED AUERBACH, C. 1980. Nate "Tiny" Archibald signs a one-year contract with the Celtics. Archibald played five seasons for the Celtics (1978–1979 to 1982–1983), which included playing on the championship team of 1981. His injury in the 1982 playoffs cost the team back-to-back world titles. (Frank O'Brien photograph, courtesy the Sports Museum.)

A 1980–1981 BRUINS PROGRAM. The Bruins newest star, Calder Cup (rookie of the year) winner Raymond Bourque graces the cover of this program. This team also included such stars as Rogie Vachon, Jean Ratelle, Wayne Cashman, Rick Middleton, Brad Park, Terry O'Reilly, and current Bruins general manager Mike O'Connell. (Courtesy the Sports Museum.)

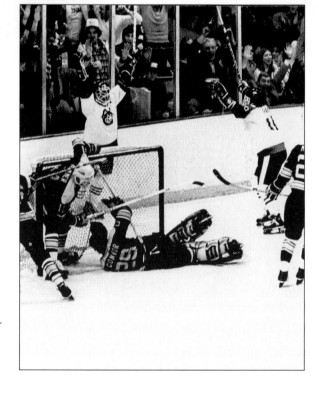

WAYNE TURNER. In a miracle finish, Wayne Turner scores in sudden-death overtime for Northeastern University to win the 1980 Beanpot. It marked the first title for the Huskies and ended a 28-year drought for the underdogs from Huntington Avenue. (Courtesy Northeastern University.)

JOHNNY MOST. Johnny Most was the voice of the Celtics for 37 seasons from 1953 until illness forced his retirement in 1990. He was a notorious "homer," and Celtics fans loved his emotional, biased, and highly entertaining style of game calling. Added to this was his distinctive voice (Johnny Most sound-alike contests are still held all over Boston), making Most as much a legend as anyone who wore the green. He died in 1993 at age 69. (Dick Raphael photograph.)

PATRICK EWING. Shown here playing for Cambridge Rindge and Latin in 1981, Jamiacan native Patrick Ewing went on to become a superstar at both Georgetown and in the NBA. Ewing honed his game at the Memorial Drive courts near his home in Cambridgeport. (Leslie H. Kimbrough photograph.)

HOOP FANS CELEBRATE. The crowd at the Boston Garden celebrates following Cambridge Rindge and Latin's win over Holy Name of Worcester. (Courtesy the Sports Museum.)

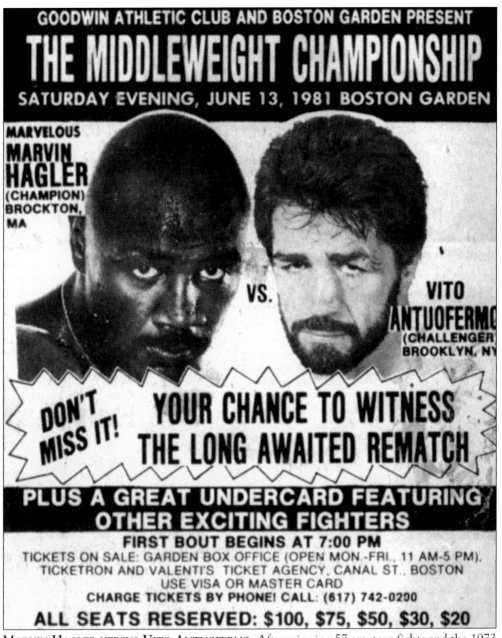

GOODWIN ATHLETIC CLUB AND BOSTON GARDEN PRESENT

THE MIDDLEWEIGHT CHAMPIONSHIP

SATURDAY EVENING, JUNE 13, 1981 BOSTON GARDEN

MARVELOUS
**MARVIN
HAGLER**
(CHAMPION)
BROCKTON,
MA

VS.

**VITO
ANTUOFERMO**
(CHALLENGER)
BROOKLYN, NY

DON'T MISS IT! **YOUR CHANCE TO WITNESS THE LONG AWAITED REMATCH**

PLUS A GREAT UNDERCARD FEATURING OTHER EXCITING FIGHTERS

FIRST BOUT BEGINS AT 7:00 PM
TICKETS ON SALE: GARDEN BOX OFFICE (OPEN MON.-FRI., 11 AM-5 PM).
TICKETRON AND VALENTI'S TICKET AGENCY, CANAL ST., BOSTON
USE VISA OR MASTER CARD
CHARGE TICKETS BY PHONE! CALL: (617) 742-0200

ALL SEATS RESERVED: $100, $75, $50, $30, $20

MARVIN HAGLER VERSUS VITO ANTUOFERMO. After winning 57 amateur fights and the 1973 Amateur Athletic Union (AAU) national middleweight championship, Brockton's Marvin Hagler became professional and won 26 consecutive bouts, including 19 by knockout. Hagler, known to all as "Marvelous Marvin," captured the world middleweight championship in London, England, on September 27, 1980, as he defeated defending champion Alan Minter with a 12th-round knockout. Elected to the International Boxing Hall of Fame, Hagler retired in 1988 to pursue an acting career. His professional record was 61 wins (51 by knockout), 3 losses, and 2 draws. (Courtesy the Sports Museum.)

ANDY MOOG AND RAY BOURQUE, C. 1992. Andy Moog came to the Bruins in a trade with Edmonton in 1988. The all-star goaltender, who won three Stanley Cups with the Oilers, played in two cup finals with Boston (1988 and 1990), ironically, against his old team. Splitting the net duties with Reggie Lemelin, they shared the Jennings Trophy (for the team with the fewest goals scored against them) in 1990. Bruins captain Ray Bourque wore the captain's C from 1988, having shared the honor with Rick Middleton following Terry O'Reilly's retirement in 1985, until his departure in 2000. (Tom Miller photograph.)

35th ANNUAL **BEANPOT**

FEBRUARY 2-9, 1987   OFFICIAL PROGRAM
BOSTON GARDEN $2.50

THE 1987 BEANPOT PROGRAM. Len Ceglarski of Boston College, Fernie Flaman of Northeastern University, Jack Parker of Boston University, and Bill Cleary of Harvard surround the Beanpot. A Boston tradition since 1952, it was originally known as the New England Invitational Hockey Tournament. The Beanpot was the brainchild of Walter Brown, president of the Boston Garden; John P. Curley of Boston College; Buff Donelli of Boston University; Bill Bingham of Harvard; and Herb Gallagher of Northeastern University. After the Boston Garden closed, the tournament moved to the FleetCenter. (Courtesy the Sports Museum.)

AEROSMITH ROCKS THE GARDEN. Steve Tyler and Joe Perry of the Boston band Aerosmith rock the old building to the rafters. (Chris Walter photograph.)

BILL RUSSELL AND K.C. JONES. Bill Russell played 13 seasons and won 11 world championships. In the 1967–1968 season, he became player-coach (succeeding Red Auerbach) until his retirement in 1969. K.C. Jones won seven straight NBA championships with the Celtics, from 1959 to 1967. He served as assistant coach on the 1981 championship team and coached two more (the 1984 and 1986 teams). (William Polo photograph, courtesy the Boston Herald.)

DENNIS JOHNSON AND LARRY BIRD. "D.J." was a durable Celtics point guard who Larry Bird claimed was the greatest player he had ever teamed with. A career 46 percent shooter from the floor with a legendary ability to hit the big shot when the team needed it, he played on championship teams in 1984 and 1986. (Courtesy Sports Action Photography.)

COACH K.C. JONES. K.C. Jones had the distinction of winning back-to-back NCAA titles at San Francisco, a gold medal in Melbourne in 1956, then seven straight NBA championships with the Celtics, from 1959 to 1967. He later won rings as assistant coach (1981) and as coach (1984 and 1986) and was elected to the Basketball Hall of Fame in 1989. (Steve Carter photograph.)

CAM NEELY, C. 1993. Cam Neely played 10 seasons with the Bruins before being forced to retire due to injuries. A three-time 50-goal scorer with a career-high 55 goals in the 1989–1990 season, he won the Masterton Trophy in 1994, the 7th Player Award in 1987, and the Dufresne Trophy in 1988, 1991, and 1994. Neely was a four-time second team all-star in 1988, 1990, 1991, and 1994. (Courtesy Sports Action Photography.)

RAY BOURQUE AND PHIL ESPOSITO, C. 1987. On the night of December 3, 1987, the Bruins honored Phil Esposito by hoisting his No. 7 to the rafters. In a surprise move, Ray Bourque (who was wearing the number) pulled off his No. 7 jersey, revealing a No. 77 jersey underneath. Bourque's 77 now hangs in the rafters along with the other Bruins retired numbers. (Courtesy Sports Action Photography.)

THE "BIG THREE." When you think of the great Celtics teams of the 1980s, you think of Kevin McHale, Robert Parish, and Larry Bird. All three played on the three world championship teams of that era (1981, 1984, and 1986). McHale and Bird played 13 seasons with the Celtics, and Parish wore the green for 14 seasons. (Tom Miller photograph.)

BRUINS GREATS ARE HONORED WITH NHL MILESTONE AWARDS. Seen here are, from left to right, Jean Ratelle, Doug Mohns, Leo Boivin, Dean Prentice, John Ziegler (NHL president), John Bucyk, Bobby Orr, Milt Schmidt, and Rick Middleton. (Courtesy the Sports Museum.)

BILL WALTON. Bill Walton was one of the game's dominant centers when healthy, but recurring foot injuries forced him to come off the bench for the Celtics. He was a productive backup to Robert Parish in the Celtics world championship season of 1986, earning the NBA's Sixth Man Award that year. (Courtesy the Sports Museum.)

Eight
THE 1990S

UNVEILING THE ORR SCULPTURE. In 1990, Armand LaMontagne's life-size sculpture of Bobby Orr was unveiled at the Boston Garden. Carved from a single block of laminated basswood, the sculpture joined an equally impressive LaMontagne statue of Larry Bird at the Sports Museum. (Courtesy the Sports Museum.)

WALT DISNEY'S WORLD ON ICE. In this production, Mickey Mouse as the sorcerer's apprentice introduces Goofy and his teenage son Max to a world of imagination—the best moments from the best Disney stories. (Courtesy the Sports Museum.)

NANCY KERRIGAN. Stoneham native and longtime Boston Garden performer Nancy Kerrigan won a silver medal for figure skating at the 1994 Olympics in Lillehammer, Norway. (Courtesy the Sports Museum.)

ROBERT PARISH. "The Chief" played 14 seasons with the Celtics, including three world championships (1981, 1984, and 1986). The nine-time NBA all-star also played for Golden State, Charlotte, and Chicago, where he won his final championship in 1997. (Steve Lipofsky photograph.)

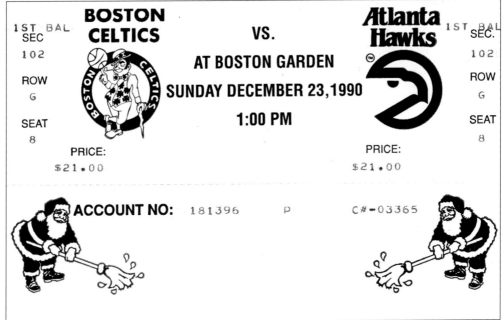

CELTICS TICKETS. These tickets were issued for a Celtics-Hawks game that had to be rescheduled due to rain leaking through the Garden roof. (Dave Cowens donation, courtesy the Sports Museum.)

ELEPHANT PARADE, C. 1990. The elephants walk from the Boston Garden to South Station to publicize the circus being in Boston. (Brian Walski photograph, courtesy the Boston Herald.)

LARRY MOULTER WITH AEROSMITH. Longtime Boston Garden president and chief executive officer Larry Moulter is shown with the Boston band Aerosmith. From left to right are Tom Hamilton, Brad Whitford, Joe Kramer, Larry Moulter, Steve Tyler, and Joe Perry. (Courtesy the Sports Museum.)

LUCIANO PAVAROTTI. World-renowned operatic virtuoso Luciano Pavarotti made a coming-out-of-retirement tour, which brought him to the Garden on November 14, 1993. This was his only New England appearance on the tour. (Courtesy the New Boston Garden Corporation.)

LARRY BIRD NIGHT. Larry Bird embraces longtime rival and friend Magic Johnson on the night his number was hoisted to the rafters, February 2, 1993. (Courtesy the Sports Museum.)

REGGIE LEWIS. Northeastern University star Reggie Lewis played for the Celtics for six seasons until his premature death in 1993. He led the Huskies to four consecutive Eastern Collegiate Athletic Conference (ECAC) North Atlantic Conference titles and was ECAC North Atlantic Conference rookie of the year in 1984. Lewis was the first-ever three-time ECAC NAC player of the year, winning in 1985, 1986, and 1987. (Steve Lipofsky photograph.)

RAY BOURQUE AND NORMAND LEVEILLE. Captain Ray Bourque helps former Bruin Normand Leveille take a last skate around the Garden. Leveille had suffered a debilitating stroke in 1983 at the beginning of a promising career. Although still partially paralyzed, he was still able to lace up for the last skate, when Bruins veterans going back to the 1930s donned vintage jerseys and took one last trip around the Garden ice. (Courtesy the Boston Bruins.)

THE TRAINERS ROOM, BOSTON GARDEN. Call it cramped, call it cozy, by the 1990s, the facilities at the Boston Garden were out of date. In this room, the Bruins training staff repaired equipment, sharpened skates, and generally kept the team going. The locker room was not much bigger, but both housed a lot of memories. (Jim Dow photograph.)

JEREMY JACOBS. Boston Bruins owner Jeremy Jacobs is also the chairman and chief executive officer Delaware North Companies, a multinational food service, recreational, and hospitality management company, one of the largest private companies in the nation. As owner of the Bruins, Jacobs represents the club on the NHL's board of governors and serves on its executive committee. (Courtesy the New Boston Garden Corporation.)

THE BOSTON GARDEN AND THE ELEVATED TRAIN. The last stretch of elevated train, part of the MBTA's Green Line, ran past the Garden's familiar spires. Decorated with a trompe l'oeil

image of painters at work, the structure will be replaced as part of Boston's Big Dig. (Courtesy the Sports Museum.)

THE BOSTON GARDEN FROM THE AIR. Soon, only the Tip O'Neill Federal Building (left) and the buildings in the foreground will remain. The Garden and 150 Causeway Street (attached

to the right) fell to the wrecker's ball. The elevated highway and Green Line will soon be replaced as part of the Big Dig. (Courtesy the Sports Museum.)

BOSTON GARDEN DEMOLITION. Because of the proximity to the expressway and the O'Neill building, the Garden had to be demolished slowly rather than imploded. The view of the half

torn-down building, its once busy interior bare and shabby, was a heart-wrenching sight for passengers on the Green Line elevated track. (Courtesy the Sports Museum.)

A NIGHT TO REMEMBER. On September 29, 1995, the Garden was retired formally with "A Night to Remember." The old building will be missed. Master of ceremonies Dan Rather hosted a program that included appearances by such sports and entertainment legends as Bobby Orr, Milt Schmidt, Woody Dumart, Larry Bird, Tom Heinsohn, John Havlicek, Tony Demarco, K.C. Jones, and Peter Wolf. (Courtesy the Sports Museum.)

OPENING NIGHT AT THE FLEETCENTER. The year 1995 marked the last season for the Boston Garden and the first for the FleetCenter. On September 30, 1995, a grand opening was held to unveil the new state-of-the-art facility. Among the artists who performed that night were the Boston Pops accompanied by Patti Labelle and James Taylor. (Courtesy the Sports Museum.)